To the Man I Love,
Thank You for Being Mine

BOOKS BY TAMARA NIKURADSE AND SCOTT MATTHEWS

To the Man I Love, Thank You for Being Mine
To the Woman I Love, Thank You for Being Mine
Dear Mom, Thank You for Being Mine
Dear Dad, Thank You for Being Mine
Stuck in the Seventies
(with Jay Kerness, Jay Steele, and Greg White)

To the Man I Love,
THANK YOU FOR
BEING MINE

Tamara Nikuradse
Scott Matthews

FAWCETT COLUMBINE / NEW YORK

A Fawcett Columbine Book
Published by Ballantine Books

Copyright © 1994 by Scott Matthews and Tamara Nikuradse

Library of Congress Catalog Card Number: 93-90741

ISBN: 0-449-90914-X

Cover design by Richard Hasselberger
Text design by Mary A. Wirth

Manufactured in the United States of America
First Edition: February 1994

10 9 8 7 6 5 4 3 2 1

Dedicated to all men,
who make these thank-yous possible.

———⊷●⊷———

ACKNOWLEDGMENTS

We'd like to thank the following couples who have been great role models for us over the years: Glenn and Gail Matthews, Brett Matthews and Ginger Salazar-Matthews, Lynne and Jim Salmon, Bruce and Gingee Thunberg, Gap and Gram Matthews, Gram Thunberg and Leo McClosky, Tanya Townes and Tim Moynihan, Alexander Nikuradse and Turbo Utta, and Charles and Odeline Townes.

Thank you to all of the people at Ballantine who brought this book to you, especially Matthew Shear and our editor, Sherri Rifkin, for their tremendous efforts. And finally, a special thank-you to Barbara Alpert and Mary Jane Ross for all their help and encouragement.

Introduction

In keeping with the spirit of our two previous books—*Dear Mom, Thank You for Being Mine* and *Dear Dad, Thank You for Being Mine*—we wanted to thank one another for the love, support, understanding, and for all the many things that we have given to each other during our twelve years together. This book is inspired by those twelve years.

We hope the following thank-yous spark special memories for you and inspire you to write your own thank-yous to the man you love. Your words and expressions of love will make this collection even more meaningful. Feel free to cross out words and personalize the thank-yous or enter your special thank-yous on the blank page at the end of the book. If some of the thank-yous written in this book do not apply to your love, and you want them to, why not drop the hint and write *(HINT . . . HINT . . .)* or *NOT!!!* after our thank-you.

We wish you lots of love, happiness, and serendipity.

Tamara and Scott

To the Man I Love,

THANK YOU ...

Thank you for noticing me and knowing it was love at first sight.

Thank you for asking me for a date instead of hitting me over the head with your club and dragging me by my hair back to your cave.

Thank you for not asking me what
my sign was or using some other corny line
about destiny that you learned from a
"How to Pick Up Babes" book.

Thank you for being
surprised when I replied, "Sure."

Thank you for being on time for our first date
and trying so hard to make it a great one.

Thank you for not considering dinner
on our first date as foreplay.

Thank you for not waiting weeks before
calling me back after our first date.

Thank you for our first mouth-watering
kiss, which I will cherish forever.

Thank you for giving pink slips to your old
girlfriends when a fortune-teller told you a
beautiful, intelligent, sophisticated, classy lady
with a great personality and an incredible pair
of legs would walk into your life.

Thank you for not being afraid of
the *C* word (Commitment) and
promoting me from friend to girlfriend.

Thank you for destroying the evidence of
your former girlfriends and erasing your
"little black computer disk" of names,
phone numbers, ratings, and digital images.

Thank you for trying to impress me by taking me to a *fancy-shmancy* French restaurant even though you couldn't read the menu.

Thank you for rowing me around a pond without splashing me or capsizing the boat.

Thank you for giving me a tour of your hometown so that I could see where you grew up.

Thank you for taking me to my favorite restaurant for greasy cheeseburgers, fries, and malted milk shakes.

Thank you for overcoming your butterflies and singing "Unforgettable" to me in front of a roomful of strangers at a karaoke bar while you were still sober.

Thank you for courting me with words
and flowers and special touches.

Thank you for commissioning a street artist
to draw my caricature—in a flattering way.

Thank you for "running out of gas"
in a secluded spot so that we could neck.

Thank you for scratching those hard-to-reach itchy spots and tickling me along the way.

Thank you for window-shopping with me and dreaming about the day when I could buy you all of the things that you desire.

Thank you for thinking of
the Heimlich maneuver when you confessed
"I love you" for the first time and
I choked on a mouthful of food.

Thank you for proposing a toast
to me and to our future together
every time we drink champagne.

Thank you for serenading me from outside the window of my apartment.

Thank you for being my Romeo— and not the kind of Romeo where I have to ask, "Wherefore art thou, Romeo?"

Thank you for showing me how to throw
a curve ball and catch a high fly.

Thank you for watching sunsets with me.

Thank you for taking me to the racetrack
to bet on the long shots.

Thank you for betting on me to place
even when your buddies, the odds makers,
rated me a long shot.

Thank you for not getting too jealous
when there's a message on my answering
machine from an old boyfriend.

Thank you for taking me to the zoo
to see the animals that resemble you.

Thank you for trying to round
second base at a drive-in movie.

Thank you for playing the combination of our birthdays in the lottery in the hope of escaping to some tropical island in the South Pacific, far from the madding crowd, where we can sip margaritas while lounging on beach chaises.

Thank you for telling me that you've already won the jackpot by having me.

Thank you for calling me every night
before you went to sleep
just to say "good night."

Thank you for being my Prince Charming.

Thank you for not being Prince Charles.

Thank you for never saying anything *too* intimate on the phone in case someone is eavesdropping.

Thank you for giving up raw onions and garlic when I entered your life.

Thank you for passing through your chewing tobacco phase before you met me.

Thank you for treating me to a hot fudge
sundae after a Saturday night movie.

Thank you for disproving the notion that
a good man is hard to find.

Thank you for those long talks
about everything and anything.

Thank you for spraying your
gushy love letters with your cologne.

Thank you for practicing
safe sex before you met me.

Thank you for waiting until
I was ready to go all the way.

Thank you for making our "first time" making
love the most incredible, indelible, edible,
delectable, and unforgettable experience ever!

Thank you for taking the
responsibility and wearing condoms.

Thank you for waking up with a sparkle
in your eyes the morning after and not with
the look of a deer whose eyes are caught
in the fog lights of an oncoming Mack Truck.

Thank you for respecting me in the morning.

Thank you for canceling your subscriptions to those men's magazines because you no longer have a reason to "read" all of those articles.

Thank you for wanting to meet my parents.

Thank you for impressing my family with all of the qualities that made me fall in love with you.

Thank you for eating whatever my Mom cooked for you and telling her it was delicious.

Thank you for sneaking into my bedroom for a little hanky-panky in the middle of the night when we stayed at my parents' house.

Thank you for not getting caught.

Thank you for warning me what to say
and what not to say to your parents
before our first meeting.

Thank you for loving me even more after I
revealed to you my deep, dark secrets.

Thank you for never betraying my trust by
revealing all of my deep, dark secrets to anyone.

Thank you for finally giving me a key to your place and my *very own* bureau drawer.

Thank you for presenting me with gift certificates for facials and manicures at my favorite salon.

Thank you for serving me a pancake breakfast in bed with a rose garnish, for no special reason.

Thank you for sparing me
the fun and adventure of all-pro wrestling
and monster truck rallies.

Thank you for fixing up some of my girlfriends with your friends.

Thank you for not holding it against me for too long when my girlfriends said your friends were butt-heads with only one thing on their minds.

Thank you for vowing never to fix up our friends again.

Thank you for not being like your buddies.

Thank you for sending me on treasure hunts and whetting my appetite with chocolate goodies leading to the "pot of gold."

Thank you for giving up the Don "Stubble" Johnson look within three years after "Miami Vice" was canceled.

Thank you for surprising me with a roast chicken dinner, complete with pan-browned potatoes, after a hard day at work—and not letting on that you bought everything already cooked at the gourmet deli.

Thank you for being as faithful as a puppy dog no matter how many women flirt with you.

Thank you for being my fluffy pillow.

Thank you for always being there
to zip and button me up.

Thank you for always being there to unzip and
unbutton me—and for the little kisses you drop
on my neck and spine as you get lower and lower.

Thank you for protecting me from big barking dogs that chase our bikes.

Thank you for carrying my tampons when I didn't have a purse.

Thank you for winking at me from across a crowded room in a secret way that signals "I love you."

Thank you for showing me the list of all
the things you'd like to do before you die
so that we can do them together.

Thank you for calling in sick for me
when I needed a mental health day and
I was too chicken to call in myself.

Thank you for cradling me until I fell asleep.

Thank you for snuggling with me at football games to keep me warm and for explaining how to score touchdowns in baseball and home runs in football and why the hockey pitchers punt after the third strike.

Thank you for keeping your eyes on the football instead of on the cheerleaders.

Thank you for going for long walks through
the woods on crisp autumn days.

Thank you for gutting a pumpkin with me
and carving a toothless jack-o'-lantern.

Thank you for baking a pumpkin pie
from the pumpkin entrails to take to
my parents' house for Thanksgiving.

Thank you for turning down our bed and placing a gold-foiled chocolate and a single rose on my pillow.

Thank you for believing me when I said, "The devil made me do it."

Thank you for pouring hot butter over
fresh popped corn and cuddling with me
on the couch to watch romantic movies
like *An Affair to Remember.*

Thank you for taking the scenic route
when we're not in a rush.

Thank you for telling my girlfriends
how much you love and adore me so that
the message will come back to me.

Thank you for blowing
bubbles with me in the park.

Thank you for your little chivalrous acts like
standing guard outside the men's room door
when I had to go to the bathroom and the line
to the women's room was too long.

Thank you for fulfilling a teen fantasy
by making love to me in the backseat of a car
at the Point in my old neighborhood.

Thank you for not drinking out of bottles
and putting them back in the fridge.

Thank you for watching *It's a Wonderful Life*
with me every Christmas.

Thank you for baking Christmas cookies
and decorating them with me.

Thank you for carrying a sprig of mistletoe in
your pocket the whole month of December so
you could whip it out at a moment's notice.

Thank you for humoring me and sitting
through *The Nutcracker* year after year.

Thank you for always knowing exactly what
I want for my gifts (and for noticing
the catalogs with the circled suggestions).

Thank you for thinking of jewelry
instead of appliances for my gifts.

Thank you for stuffing my
stocking with decadent goodies.

Thank you for dressing up in a red suit and being my Santa . . . *Ho! Ho! Ho!*

Thank you for celebrating our very own Christmas before we visited our relatives.

Thank you for kissing me when the clock struck 12 to bring in the New Year.

Thank you for not breaking
too many of your New Year's resolutions
by the second week in January.

Thank you for making angels
in the snow with me.

Thank you for building a fire in the fireplace and
dimming the lights on a cold winter's night.

Thank you for chasing away
the winter blahs with your warm smiles.

Thank you for always being my Saturday
night date even if we just stay home and
veg like couch potatoes in front of the TV.

Thank you for making every
Thursday a candlelight pizza night.

Thank you for explaining
that your two kings and two queens
beat my four sevens in strip poker.

Thank you for composing a love poem
for me that almost rhymes and doesn't
begin with "Roses are red . . ."

Thank you for closing your eyes when we kiss.

Thank you for ordering in Chinese
and feeding me with chopsticks.

Thank you for holding me
when I needed to be held.

Thank you for loving every square inch of me from head to toe—even my problem areas.

Thank you for asking me to be your Valentine with a dozen long-stem roses and sexy lingerie from Victoria's Secret.

Thank you for getting frisky with me between the red satin sheets.

Thank you for celebrating Valentine's Day 365 days of the year.

Thank you for devising the most romantic way to propose to me and keeping it a secret.

Thank you for taking the hint from Marilyn when she sang about diamonds being a girl's best friend and buying me the most beautiful ring in the world.

Thank you for making my Dad's day by asking for my hand in marriage.

Thank you for getting
his joke when he said, "No!"

Thank you for surviving my father's third degree
when he interrogated you about your intentions.

Thank you for saving me
from a life of spinsterhood.

Thank you for giving me the best incentive to
lose weight—a wedding dress in six months.

Thank you for being my genie
and granting me three wishes.

Thank you for granting my first wish
when you said you would marry me.

Thank you for granting my second wish when you
said you'd spend the rest of your life with me.

Thank you for granting my third wish when you
said you'd be the father of our children.

Thank you for asking me to dance even
though you really don't like dancing.

Thank you for speculating with me what will happen
in the next Taster's Choice coffee commercial.

Thank you for forbidden pleasures like a *ménage à
trois* with you, me, and Mr. Bubble.

Thank you for letting me open the prizes at
the bottom of the Cracker Jack boxes.

Thank you for not bringing home
a Chia Pet when I asked for a cat.

Thank you for surprising me with
a kitten decorated with a red bow as a
"just because I love you" gift.

Thank you for growing to tolerate
my precious kitty cat, Black Beauty, even though
you like dogs better than cats.

Thank you for not teasing
the nine lives out of Black Beauty.

Thank you for not starving Black Beauty
when I'm away on business trips.

Thank you for cleaning out Black Beauty's litter box.

Thank you for finally understanding that
I don't love my cat more than I love you.
(I love you both in equal amounts.)

Thank you for sending me on
an Easter egg hunt where you substituted
bath beads for jelly beans and
scented soaps for marshmallow rabbits.

Thank you for exchanging
"I" for "we."

Thank you for making passionate love to me.

Thank you for encouraging me
to have girls' nights out.

Thank you for not acting like a teenager
in heat during your nights out with the guys.

Thank you for stopping to watch
street performers and donating your
loose change for the performance.

Thank you for closing the umbrella, singing
in the rain, and jumping in puddles with me.

Thank you for the unexpected
bouquet of flowers (even if you picked it
from our neighbor's yard).

Thank you for getting all of your friends
to help us move into our first place together.

Thank you for sending a card to my mother
on Mother's Day thanking her for creating me.

Thank you for catching me at the bottom
of a slide and not jumping off the seesaw
when I was still on the other end.

Thank you for renting a convertible and cruising
along a coastal highway with me.

Thank you for flagging down the ice cream truck
and buying me my favorite ice cream.

Thank you for being my electric blanket
when you blast the air conditioner.

Thank you for rubbing SPF 15 suntan lotion on my back and not letting your hands stray too far off course (well, sometimes . . .).

Thank you for finding my bikini top after an unfortunate body surfing accident.

Thank you for not dragging me,
kicking and screaming, into cold water.

Thank you for making me see
fireworks when you kiss me—even when
it's not the Fourth of July.

Thank you for keeping your eyes in your sockets and not leering at other women, especially those who wear thongs (and look good) on the beach.

Thank you for not expecting *me*
to wear a thong on a beach.

Thank you for not wearing a skimpy Speedo on the beach that accentuates your family jewels.

Thank you for burying me
from neck to toe in the sand.

Thank you for digging me out.

Thank you for dancing barefoot with me
under the stars on a cool summer's night.

Thank you for being a gentleman even
when you're not around my parents.

Thank you for not setting a stopwatch
when I enter a store to shop for clothes.

Thank you for driving with me
as if you're carrying precious cargo.

Thank you for keeping your machismo
in check by not flipping the bird at some guy
who cuts you off and chasing his car down the
highway so that you can avenge this wrong.

Thank you for swallowing your male ego and
finally pulling over to ask for directions instead
of driving around for another hour trying
to find the way yourself.

Thank you for putting the Sunday papers
back in some semblance of order
before giving them to me.

Thank you for washing my hair in the sink without
getting the shampoo in my eyes.

Thank you for displaying your signs of affection in
public and for not getting too carried away.

Thank you for giving me my "space"
when I needed time alone.

Thank you for learning new tricks
despite being an old dog.

Thank you for knowing the right names—
Gap, J. Crew, Talbots, Ann Taylor . . .

Thank you for sensing when I needed you without my having to tell you.

Thank you for not recycling lame excuses like "I forgot" or "I didn't hear you."

Thank you for carrying a flattering photo of me in your wallet with all of my vital statistics written on the back (i.e., ring size, bra size, dress size, birth date, etc.).

Thank you for not expecting me to have a Barbie doll's measurements, just like I don't expect you to have G.I. Joe's physique.

Thank you for not snapping a picture of me in the shower.

Thank you for growing facial hair
on demand.

Thank you for not giving me
beard burn.

Thank you for shaving facial hair
on demand.

Thank you for not canceling the wedding
after the 1,293 fights over the smallest details,
like the right shade of white for the wedding
invitations, having tails or no tails
for the groomsmen, whether or not to seat
your single aunt at the table with the most
eligible bachelors, your mother's involvement . . .

Thank you for not touching the "entertainment" during your bachelor party.

Thank you for not waking up in a different state the morning after your bachelor party.

Thank you for not expecting a dowry or my parents to pay for the wedding.

Thank you for not making
your dog the best man.

Thank you for showing up at the altar
on time and without a hangover.

Thank you for vowing to love,
honor, cherish, and *obey* me.

Thank you for crying tears
of joy during the ceremony.

Thank you for making me a bride at last!

Thank you for not
getting drunk at our reception.

Thank you for not stepping
on my dress during our first dance.

Thank you for not belting the photographer after
he said "Say cheese" for the 416th time.

Thank you for making our wedding day
the happiest day of my life.

Thank you for keeping the destination
of our honeymoon a complete surprise until
we arrived at the departure gate.

Thank you for studying *How to Satisfy a Woman <u>Every Time</u>* before the honeymoon.

Thank you for doing just that.

Thank you for our spare-no-expense, run-up-the-debt, all-night-romps-in-the-bed honeymoon.

Thank you for never letting our honeymoon end.

Thank you for calling my mom "Mom."

Thank you for trying to convince my parents that they are not losing a daughter, they're gaining a son.

Thank you for wanting a family portrait
of just the two of us.

Thank you for understanding that
granny pj's (while less sexy) are a lot
more comfortable to sleep in than all those frilly,
lacy little things that barely cover my derrière.

Thank you for agreeing to do at least
50 percent of the housework.

Thank you for forking over the money
a week later to pay for a cleaning person
when you failed to do your 50 percent.

Thank you for paying the Social Security
tax for our cleaning person in case
I run for public office in the future.

Thank you for not keeping score on
who gives in and who doesn't.

Thank you for not calling me your little
woman or old lady or ball and chain.

Thank you for asking about my day.

Thank you for revealing your fantasies
to me (and acting them out with me).

Thank you for draping your jacket
over me when I felt a chill.

Thank you for making goofy faces
to keep me from crying.

Thank you for not purchasing products
featured in infomercials.

Thank you for not killing the plants
when I asked you to water them.

Thank you for always celebrating the anniversary
of our first kiss.

Thank you for not getting complacent about
our relationship or taking me for granted.

Thank you for teaching me curse words
in different languages.

Thank you for not using any of your
curse words on me within earshot.

Thank you for comforting
me after my nightmare.

Thank you for indulging in eating orgies
with me when I am down and out.

Thank you for dieting with me to lose
those extra pounds after our eating orgies.

Thank you for believing that abstinence
makes the heart grow fonder while
you're away on business.

Thank you for keeping a framed picture
of me on your desk.

Thank you for engaging in intelligent discussions with me.

Thank you for taking an active role in our birth control.

Thank you for finding my
E, F, and G spots.

Thank you for your passion.

Thank you for sharing a
common definition of foreplay.

Thank you for not rolling over to fall
asleep directly after making love and for
not asking, "Was it good for you?"

Thank you for pillow-talking with me and
holding me tight as we drift off to sleep.

Thank you for reading my women's magazines to better understand the superior sex.

Thank you for flattering my mom by asking her if she lost weight.

Thank you for picking out
my strands of gray hair.

Thank you for noticing my change in
hair style or hair color within 24 hours and
saying you love it, without wincing.

Thank you for eating a little less fat and a little less
salt, because you want to grow old with me.

Thank you for not hesitating
to ask for my help or opinion.

Thank you for wearing your
wedding ring even though your buddies don't.

Thank you for letting me sleep
in your T-shirts and sweatshirts.

Thank you for putting the cap
back on the toothpaste tube.

Thank you for not wearing a
pinky ring and seven pounds of gold chains.

Thank you for not saying
"ciao" instead of "good-bye."

Thank you for keeping me on my toes
with your practical jokes.

Thank you for buying a car
with dual-side air bags.

Thank you for not scratching or
playing with your "package" in public.

Thank you for adoring children.

Thank you for those incredible
bear hugs that nearly suffocate me.

Thank you for tucking me in at night.

Thank you for not spending your
every waking hour on a bar stool and talking
about me the way Norm talks about Vera.

Thank you for being my very own
life-size *Playgirl* centerfold.

Thank you for not commanding me
to fetch a beer from the fridge.

Thank you for planting a tree as a symbol
of your love—virile, fertile, and erect.

Thank you for being in touch with your
feelings and not being afraid to cry.

Thank you for telling me how beautiful
I am when I feel so ugly.

Thank you for being generous
when we make love.

Thank you for not bragging about my performance in the sack to your buddies.

Thank you for your tender touch that caresses my hand each time it meets yours.

Thank you for attending ballroom dance classes with me and not stepping on my toes too often.

Thank you for not laughing at me
when I'm using the ThighMaster™.

Thank you for opening the really stuck jar lids.

Thank you for not smudging
my makeup with sloppy kisses.

Thank you for not pulling a Schwarzenegger by flexing your muscles in my face and expecting me to glory in your manliness.

Thank you for giving me that special medicine called "love" that no doctor could prescribe and no pharmacist could bottle, label, and mark up the price for.

Thank you for not giving me reasons to run away
with my friends Thelma and Louise.

Thank you for checking with
Black Beauty and me before you brought home
a mutt from the ASPCA.

Thank you for not getting too mad
when the Talbots bill arrived.

Thank you for letting me borrow your boxer shorts, dress shirts, T-shirts, clean tube socks . . .

Thank you for letting me keep your boxer shorts, dress shirts, T-shirts, tube socks . . .

Thank you for not taking me to places with signs that read: "Ladies Welcome."

Thank you for knowing the difference between an endive and an end dive.

Thank you for discussing personal investment strategies with me.

Thank you for not wearing socks with holes
in them when we go shoe shopping.

Thank you for insisting that I've lost weight when
I've actually gained a few pounds.

Thank you for waiting in a long line with me
at the movie theater for a "chick flick"
that you didn't want to see.

Thank you for always making me feel desirable.

Thank you for not teasing me
with creepy crawly bugs.

Thank you for celebrating
my pay raises and promotions.

Thank you for being respectful of the neighbors
and not moaning too loud.

Thank you for being a feminist, even though you
don't think you are one.

Thank you for not wishing that I looked
like some anorexic, music-video vixen with
implants and an obvious dye job.

 T hank you for not peeking at my diary to see what
interesting things I write about you.

 T hank you for not whining like a spoiled mama's
boy and stomping in the aisles of a
store when you don't get your way.

Thank you for patiently waiting those *few* extra minutes as I blow-dried and curled my hair, applied makeup, selected an outfit, reselected another outfit, and put on the right accessories just to go to the grocery store.

Thank you for patiently waiting those *few* extra minutes as I brushed my hair, wiped off my makeup, moisturized my face, and slipped on a nightie just to go to bed.

Thank you for bringing me two aspirin when I said, "Not tonight, honey, I have a headache."

Thank you for not kicking Black Beauty off the bed when we make love.

Thank you for taking night classes with me.

Thank you for not telling me that
a woman's place is in the kitchen.

Thank you for not revealing my age to others,
because they'd accuse you of robbing the cradle.

Thank you for giving me the pleasure
of hearing your voice on my voice mail.

Thank you for taking vitamin E to help you rise to the occasion.

Thank you for supporting my career and understanding when I have to travel or work late.

Thank you for helping to build our retirement nest egg by diversifying our eggs.

Thank you for appreciating the magic
of push-up bras.

Thank you for calling me at work
to whisper sweet nothings in my ear.

Thank you for opening doors and pulling
out chairs for me and not caring
if it's politically correct or not.

Thank you for warming your hands before coming
to bed and touching my warm skin.

Thank you for treating me to an
aromatherapy massage at a spa.

Thank you for not spending
every Sunday afternoon polishing
your car or watching ball games.

Thank you for loving me more than your car.

Thank you for not letting it go in
one ear and out the other.

Thank you for not eating crackers in bed.

Thank you for ironing my shirt
because I was in a rush.

Thank you for saying "I love the outfit"
instead of "How much?" when you
see me in something new.

Thank you for buying me gifts that
I will use more than you will.

Thank you for being
my Pictionary® game partner.

Thank you for escorting me
to my school reunions and not laughing
at my old boyfriends who are balding
and have third-trimester paunches.

Thank you for telling me that
with every new day I grow more beautiful.

Thank you for understanding
when "No!" means "No!"

Thank you for understanding when
"Nooooooooh" means "Yes!"

Thank you for not throwing away
the mail-order catalogs before I
have a chance to order from them.

Thank you for turning off the alarm clock
even though you had to reach across me
because I was too lazy to reach for it myself.

Thank you for not frequenting
strip bars with the boys after work.

Thank you for name-dropping
at the appropriate moments (i.e.,
"I have to check with my wife.").

Thank you for cleaning spaghetti
splatter from the stove top.

Thank you for telling me that
you wouldn't let Robert Redford sleep with me
for all the money in the world.

Thank you for spending Saturdays
hunting for our dream house.

Thank you for listening to me
when I need to talk.

Thank you for teaching me how
to make a real cup of coffee.

Thank you for not breaking any of my Engelbert
Humperdinck or Barry Manilow albums when I
insisted on playing them over and over again.

Thank you for not expecting my career
to take a backseat to yours.

Thank you for not draping your arm around
me like a "No Trespassing" sign.

Thank you for knowing all of my favorites:
color, dessert, food, precious stone . . .

Thank you for massaging the stress knots out of my
back when I arrived home after a *BAD* day.

Thank you for not longing
to appear on "Studs."

Thank you for brushing my hair until it shines.

Thank you for not telling me "I told you so" when I
overpacked my suitcase and you
had to lug it through the airport.

Thank you for pumping up the volume
and blasting the good songs.

Thank you for respecting my privacy by not
reading my mail or eavesdropping on my phone
conversations no matter how tempted you are.

Thank you for trying to stay in shape.

Thank you for hanging up your wet towels
instead of letting them mildew in a corner.

Thank you for buying me Mace—just in case.

Thank you for making a surprise guest appearance in my shower.

Thank you for understanding that,
when I say I'll be back from the
beauty salon in two hours,
I really mean five hours.

Thank you for loving my parents
and thinking of them as friends.

Thank you for playing handyman around
the house and fixing things.

Thank you for not using handyman lingo
and referring to making love as screwing,
chiseling, hammering, or nailing.

Thank you for letting me play
with your power tools.

Thank you for never telling
me the honeymoon's over.

Thank you for promising that when you even-
tually lose your hair you won't comb the
remaining few strands over your scalp.

Thank you for easing my worries
by calling me when you're going to be late.

Thank you for not comparing me
to your old girlfriends.

Thank you for not leaving
a bar of soap in the bottom of the tub.

Thank you for saving
all of my love letters to you.

Thank you for not complaining
about my hand-washed undergarments
drying all over the bathroom.

Thank you for not needing to find your primal
self by running off to the woods to beat drums
with half-clad men once a month.

Thank you for offering the last cookie
in the cookie jar to me first.

Thank you for giving me your old fishing-
tackle box to store my makeup.

Thank you for not doing something
where you have to say, "I was only kidding!"

Thank you for acting really surprised when you walked into a room filled with your friends for your surprise birthday party.

Thank you for not harboring any dark secrets like a fetish for cross-dressing.

Thank you for caring about things that I care about.

Thank you for admitting your mistakes
and not reincarnating my mistakes.

Thank you for explaining why
the Three Stooges are funny.

Thank you for not snapping my bra.

Thank you for faxing fun cartoons
and notes to me at work.

Thank you for not leaving your smelly
old sneakers in my olfactory radius.

Thank you for making me feel special
(and my co-workers envious) by sending flowers
to me at work.

Thank you for teaching me
how to jump-start a car.

Thank you for waiting until I was done eating before you started to pick off my plate.

Thank you for inspiring me with your pep talks.

Thank you for making my friends your friends.

 Thank you for excusing yourself when frothy
flatulence or belly belches emit from your body.

 Thank you for pouring the congealed milk from
the fridge down the drain every month or so.

Thank you for sending me a customized
Vermont Teddy Bear that resembles you so
that I have something to hug when
you're away on business trips.

Thank you for being open to new challenges.

Thank you for not going to bed mad at me.

$\longrightarrow$╼∋●ᘓ╾

Thank you for scaring away my hiccups.

Thank you for giving me monthly breast
exams that lead to full physicals.

Thank you for hiding in the bedroom
all night when I held a baby shower
for a friend in our living room.

Thank you for painting my toenails and waiting
until they dried before you tickled me.

Thank you for not having "MOM"
tattooed on your bicep.

Thank you for being there at the end of
"one of those days" and reminding me
of all the good things we have like
our health, our family, our love, each other.

Thank you for skipping a softball game
just so that you can spend time with me.

Thank you for indulging my sweet tooth
with Godiva chocolates.

Thank you for lifting the toilet seat before you go.

Thank you for dropping the toilet seat after you go.

Thank you for wiping the floor when you miss.

Thank you for flushing the toilet
(when I'm not in the shower).

Thank you for replacing the empty roll
of toilet paper and not leaving me stranded.

Thank you for showing me that
you care by dropping your spare change
in a homeless person's cup.

Thank you for not expecting me
to sacrifice my dreams for you but instead
to make you a part of my dreams.

Thank you for taping "Oprah" and "Donahue"
when I forget to set the VCR timer.

Thank you for not saying "it's nothing"
instead of telling me what's wrong.

Thank you for not hibernating in front
of the TV during your favorite sports seasons.

Thank you for not acting like Al Bundy,
Homer Simpson, or Beavis and Butt-head.

Thank you for not forgetting our anniversaries, especially when I've highlighted them for you on a calendar.

Thank you for clipping your nose and ear hairs.

Thank you for satisfying your exhibitionist tendencies at home by wearing a trench coat and flashing me.

Thank you for not expecting a reward, like a
barking seal, every time you perform a chore.

Thank you for not draining out
our bank account after falling
for some get-rich-quick scheme.

Thank you for not reliving in great
detail the agony you suffered just to buy me
tampons in a Quik-e-Mart.

Thank you for not moaning another
woman's name when we make love.

Thank you for not zapping the channels
with the remote (hint . . . hint).

Thank you for not zapping *me* with the "mute"
button when you didn't want to hear my voice.

Thank you for letting me zap the channel
whenever Madonna is on TV.

Thank you for speaking to my mother on the
phone even though you didn't want to.

Thank you for properly disposing of your
toenail clippings and putting the scissors
back in the proper place.

Thank you for not being too grossed out
by what you find wrapped in tissue and
discarded in the bathroom wastebasket.

Thank you for not
popping my bubble-gum bubbles.

Thank you for not hogging the blankets
and kicking me out of bed.

Thank you for not patronizing me
by saying, "Yes, dear. Yes, dear."

Thank you for not expecting an answer
when you ask, "What's for dinner?"

Thank you for not yelling questions
from the other side of the house and then
getting mad when I don't hear you.

Thank you for spraying air freshener after you use
the bathroom for protracted periods of time.

Thank you for not wearing small T-shirts that expose the bottom half of your belly.

Thank you for watching romantic Hepburn and Tracy movies on a Sunday afternoon—during commercial breaks in the ball games, that is!

Thank you for not getting *too* jealous
when other men talk to me or accusing me
of flirting with some guy.

Thank you for letting me drive *my*
car every once in a while.

Thank you for finally throwing out
your holey underwear and socks.

Thank you for not comparing me to
my mom or expecting me to be your mom.

Thank you for not doing anything that would
qualify you for a guest spot on "Geraldo."

Thank you for not ogling those lingerie-clad
models in the Victoria's Secret catalogs—
at least when I'm around.

Thank you for keeping your distance (at least 300 feet) during that time of the month.

Thank you for tolerating my mood swings—no matter what time of month.

Thank you for not believing all those time-of-the-month stories.

Thank you for being relieved when my "friend" makes its monthly visit.

Thank you for always knowing what's
wrong when you see me cry.

Thank you for admitting that you don't know
something instead of pretending that you do.

Thank you for sinking more putts with me
than on the golf course.

Thank you for not getting mad at me
when I tell you bald is sexy.

Thank you for letting me
play with your love handles.

Thank you for not licking all of the
chocolate sprinkles off my ice cream cone.

Thank you for not
tuning me out when I talk to you.

I said!

Thank you for not
tuning me out when I talk to you.

Thank you for plucking
the unibrow between your eyes.

Thank you for loaning me your razor
so that I can shave my legs and underarms.

Thank you for not
spitting in public (or private).

Thank you for telling me that I still
excite you after all these years.

Thank you for not snoring like a chain saw.

Thank you for letting me use
your favorite baseball cap on bad-hair days.

Thank you for not being afraid of intimacy.

Thank you for picking up the trail
of clothes that seems to follow you.

Thank you for never telling me,
"A man's gotta do what a man's gotta do."

Thank you for always
being there when I needed you.

Thank you for meaning it
when you say, "I'm sorry."

Thank you for being my champion.

Thank you for confiding your fears to me.

Thank you for supporting me
no matter what I do.

Thank you for keeping me sane.

Thank you for discovering new worlds with me.

Thank you for not stomping on my dreams.

Thank you for not taking me for granted.

Thank you for being the perfect mate in this life, as well as in prior and future lives.

Thank you for making me your number-one priority.

Thank you for not raining on my parades.

Thank you for *really* listening to me.

Thank you for not betraying my trust in you.

Thank you for providing me
with unconditional love.

Thank you for being my *bestest* friend
in the whole wide world.

Thank you for making a commitment to us.

Thank you for your sensitivity.

Thank you for your fidelity.

Thank you for being the yin to my yang.

Thank you for all of the fun times.

Thank you for putting my needs
ahead of your own.

Thank you for only having eyes for me.

Thank you for telling me that
"I'd like a daughter just like you."

Thank you for smiling every time you see me.

Thank you for waiting all of your life for me.

Thank you for starting our own traditions.

Thank you for telling me
that time began when you met me.

Thank you for being you.

Thank you for being mine—
always and forever.

Special Thank-Yous Just for the Man I Love

Thank you _____

_____

Thank you _____

_____

Thank you _____

_____

Thank you _____

_____

Thank you _____

_____

About the Authors

TAMARA NIKURADSE and SCOTT MATTHEWS are married and live with their three cats, Black Beauty, Lisa, and Dog Meat.

The happy couple is expecting a puppy any day now.

After *Dear Mom, Thank You for Being Mine* and *Dear Dad, Thank You for Being Mine* were published, we received many original thank-yous that people wrote for their parents, and we enjoyed reading them. If you have a special thank-you for the man or woman you love that you'd like to share, please send it to:

SCOTT MATTHEWS AND TAMARA NIKURADSE

c/o BALLANTINE BOOKS

201 EAST 50TH STREET

NEW YORK, NY 10022

Please include your name and address so that we can give you credit if we use your thank-yous in future editions.

Thank you.

DON'T FORGET THE WOMAN YOU LOVE!

- Thank you for not being a "fatal attraction."
- Thank you for living with my "little" idiosyncrasies, like my urge to zap 62 TV channels in 22 seconds flat.
- Thank you for relinquishing control of the barbecue to me, "King Potentate of All Barbecues, Master of All Grills."
- Thank you for replying, "Infinity divided by one over infinity all to the infinite power," when I ask you, "How much do you love me?"

To the Woman I Love, Thank You for Being Mine—
ask for it at your favorite bookstore.